SCIENCE IN ACTION

Water, Water!

By Tom Johnston
Illustrated by Sarah Pooley

Gareth Stevens Publishing
Milwaukee

Library of Congress Cataloging-in-Publication Data

Johnston, Tom.
  Water, water!

  (Science in action)
  Rev. ed. of: Let's imagine, water. 1985.
  Includes index.
  Summary: Demonstrates the many uses of water, where it comes from, how it is wasted, and why it is vital to the survival of living things.
  1. Water--Juvenile literature. (1. Water) I. Pooley, Sarah, ill. II. Johnston, Tom. Let's imagine, water. III. Title. IV. Series: Science in action (Milwaukee, Wis.)
  GB662.3.J64 1988   553.7   87-42750
  ISBN 1-55532-432-0
  ISBN 1-55532-407-X (lib. bdg.)

North American edition first published in 1988 by

Gareth Stevens, Inc.   7317 West Green Tree Road
Milwaukee, Wisconsin 53223, USA

This US edition copyright © 1988. First published as *Let's Imagine: Water* in the United Kingdom by The Bodley Head, London.

Text copyright © 1985 Tom Johnston
Illustrations copyright © 1985 Sarah Pooley

Hand lettering: Kathy Hall
Typeset by Web Tech, Milwaukee
Project editor: Rhoda Sherwood

Technical consultants: Jonathan Knopp, Chair, Science Department, Rufus King High School, Milwaukee; Willette Knopp, Reading Specialist and Elementary Teacher, Fox Point-Bayside (Wis.) School District.

2 3 4 5 6 7 8 9 93 92 91 90 89 88

70% of the Earth's surface is covered in water!

Imagine a world without water. That would be a world without animals, without plants, without you! All life on our planet needs water to survive.

When drought occurs, which it does frequently in the semi-arid Sahel in Africa, disaster strikes.

plants wither and die

rivers and lakes dry up

animals die

DROUGHT

The land can no longer sustain plants, so many people and animals may die of starvation and thirst.

You and I are 2/3 water. We need 2.5 quarts (2 liters) of water a day. Without this, we would die in a week.

Many plants are 80% water, and all plants need water to keep growing. The desert cactus, however, needs very little!

Whoops, forgot to water the plants. Good thing the rest are cacti!

But animals who usually live in the desert, like Tommy, my kangaroo rat, have adapted ways of surviving without water.

3

A lot of our food is made of water!

50-70%

70%

35%

Sunflower seeds are the driest food you can eat. They are only 5% water.

We need water for drinking, cooking, washing ourselves and our belongings, flushing the toilet, and watering plants.

Flushing a toilet tank uses an amazing 10.6 quarts (10 liters) of water!

SPLASH

What's the difference between a bath and a shower?

About 51 quarts (48 liters)

Showers save energy!

We also use lots of water to make electricity. In industrialized countries, making electricity can take about 40 per cent of the country's water supply. Industry also uses up a huge amount of water, since many things need surprisingly large amounts of water to be made. Making a new car, for example, uses about 530,000 quarts (500,000 l) of water, while a ton of steel uses over 262 cubic yards (200 cubic m) of water to make it.

A gallon of beer needs 19 - 48 quarts (18-45 liters) of water.

The newsprint for the daily paper uses 9.5 quarts (9 liters) of water.

Destructive waves caused by storms or by wind plus spring tides are called "tidal waves." Destructive waves caused by earthquakes or volcanos under the ocean are called "tsunamis."

BEFORE

AFTER

Tsunamis can cause lots of damage, and sometimes many people drown.

So water is an important part of our lives, and we use and waste a large amount of it. But where does all this water come from, and where does it go to when we have finished with it?

Let's start by looking at the places where we find the largest amounts of water. These are the seas and lakes. One of the first things you notice about large areas of water is that they usually have waves on them. You can make your own waves in a bath or a bowl of water. This experiment works best if you use a shallow bath and switch an overhead light on. Watch the shadow patterns the waves make on the bottom of the bath.

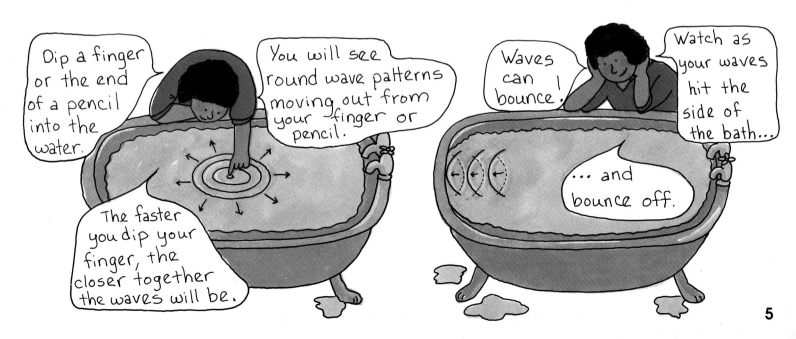

Dip a finger or the end of a pencil into the water.

You will see round wave patterns moving out from your finger or pencil.

The faster you dip your finger, the closer together the waves will be.

Waves can bounce!

Watch as your waves hit the side of the bath...

... and bounce off.

5

If you live near a pond you have probably made waves on it by throwing in stones. You may even have lost a ball in a pond and tried to get it back by throwing sticks near it. This doesn't work very well, since the ball seems to move up and down on the waves rather than along with them. Although the waves appear to move along the surface of the pond, the water is really moving up and down in one place. Usually it is the wind blowing on the surface of the water that makes waves. On a windless day even the sea can be completely flat and calm.

In France they have found a way of using the tide to produce energy by building a dam across the mouth of the Rance River. As the tide comes in and goes out across this dam, it produces hydroelectric power, electricity from moving water. Suggestions have been put forward to do this across the Severn River, near Bristol, in Britain. Scientists are working on other ways of taking power from waves and tides to give us a safe, everlasting source of energy.

Tidal power stations are very cheap to run, but they cost a lot to build.

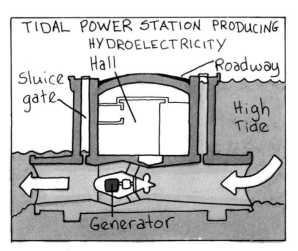

TIDAL POWER STATION PRODUCING HYDROELECTRICITY

Hall

Sluice gate

Roadway

High Tide

Generator

Not many sites are suitable for tidal power stations. They can be built only where there is a large rise and fall in water levels caused by the tides.

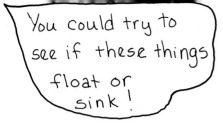

You could try to see if these things float or sink!

A coin

An orange

A plastic boat

A full lemonade bottle

A glass tumbler

We also use the sea to move lots of materials around the world on ships. It's just as well that things can float on water. Have you ever wondered why it is that some things float and others sink? You may have thought that light objects float and heavy objects sink. If you try floating lots of different things in a bowl of water, you will find that some light objects sink, while some heavy ones float. It can't therefore be just weight that makes things sink. So what is it that makes objects float?

When you go swimming, you may have noticed that you seem to be lighter than usual. You seem to weigh less in the water than you do out of it. If you try to lift up a friend in the swimming pool, he or she will feel very light — at least until well out of the water, that is!

We call this effect of things being lighter in water buoyancy, and it helps to explain why things float.

And an empty one!

A dinner plate

empty one!

A bar of soap

A pencil

But if the egg is bad... it will float!

If the egg is fresh... it sinks!

Try any other objects you can think of!

Try the egg test!

8

When you put any object into water, it pushes some of the water out of the way, displaces it. This idea of objects in water displacing some of the water and then seeming to weigh less is called "Archimedes' principle."

Archimedes was a Greek who spent most of his life studying science. He lived from 287-212 BC. A story is told of how he discovered why things float. It is said that he sat in his bath one day and watched the water spill over the sides. He is then supposed to have run naked through the streets yelling, "Eureka!" This is Greek for "I've found it!"

You and Archimedes aren't the only animals that displace water. Fish do it all the time. They show a clever use of the "Archimedes' principle" whenever they rise or dive in the water. Inside a fish is a sac called a swim bladder, which the fish can fill or empty with air. When the swim bladder is full of air, the fish rises in the water because it is more buoyant, displaces more water. When the swim bladder has less air in it, the fish becomes smaller and less buoyant, displaces less water. It then sinks in the water.

A submarine works in a similar way, but instead of a swim bladder it has ballast tanks that can be filled with air to make it float or water to make it dive. You can make your own submarine:

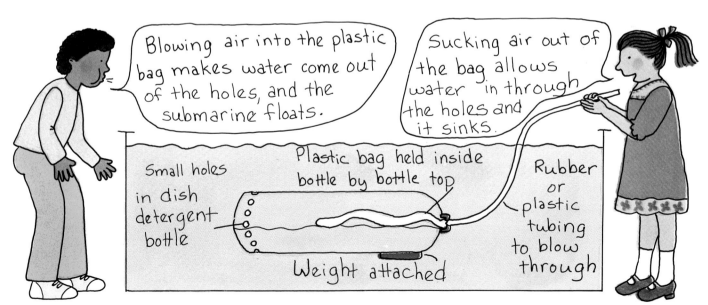

Submarines can be useful for exploring under the sea. They have even gone under the ice at the North Pole. The ice, of course, is floating on the water. When water freezes, becoming ice, it expands, pushes aside its own weight of water, and floats. If you ever see an iceberg, four-fifths of it would be under the surface displacing the water. You can try this out for yourself on a smaller scale by floating an ice cube in a glass of water.

Remember to ask someone before you use up all the salt.

Things float better in salty water. Try this experiment to see for yourself.

① Float a bottle in a bucket of water. A little sand at the bottom will make the bottle float upright.

Mark where the water level is on the side of the bottle.

② Now add lots of salt to the water and stir it to make it dissolve. Float the bottle again.

The bottle should float higher in the water.

All sea water is salty so it is easier to swim in than rivers or lakes. If you boil a pan of sea water until it's almost dry, you will find salt left behind on the sides of the pan. The Dead Sea is very salty, so you would float higher in the water there than you would in fresh water.

The Dead Sea in Jordan would be a great place to learn to swim. You couldn't possibly sink there.

I bet you thought it was a whale. No it's me, Unsinkable Susan.

13

Ships have to sail through both the salt water of seas and the fresh water of rivers. You may have seen a strange series of lines painted on the sides of large ships. These are called Plimsoll lines. They show the depth to which a ship can be safely loaded in different types of water without capsizing.

If you leave a jar of salt open, the salt gets damp.

That's because the salt takes water vapor out of the air.

All the water we use starts off in the sea, but it doesn't taste salty when it comes out of our taps. So what happens to it in the meantime?

Water from the sea, and any other water exposed to the air, is slowly evaporating. This means that the water is turning into a gas in the air. Even though you cannot see it, the air always has water in it. We call this water vapor.

If you want to dry wet clothes, hang them out.

The water from them evaporates into the air.

Even humans can dry themselves like this, but it might take a long time.

I needed a bath.

Fill a bowl to the brim with water and leave it outside. Go back every hour and mark the level of the water with a felt-tip pen. The level should drop as the water evaporates into the air. Try this on a hot day and a cold one to see if it makes any difference.

I needed a drink.

TWEET! TWEET!

Be sure there are no animals around when you do this experiment.

15

The most consistently rainy place in the world is Mt. Waialeale, in the Hawaiian islands.

Rain falls 350 days a year.

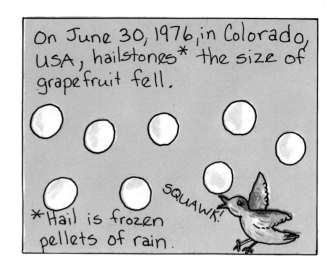

On June 30, 1976, in Colorado, USA, hailstones* the size of grapefruit fell.

SQUAWK!

*Hail is frozen pellets of rain.

Clouds are made up of tiny droplets of water that have formed around small pieces of dust high up in the sky. When some of the larger drops of water fall from the clouds, we call it rain. In winter, it falls as hail or snow.

The raindrops may fall onto the land and collect together to give us streams and rivers. Before any of this water reaches our taps, a number of interesting things can happen to it.

At Acapulco, Mexico, a fall of maggots accompanied a rainstorm on October 5, 1968.

The maggots must have been sucked up by vertical winds into a shower cloud.

In India every year torrential monsoon rains fall, sometimes resulting in floods.

People are made homeless and often many drown.

Acid rain occurs when air is polluted with sulfuric and nitric acids from factories. Acid rain attacks forests, lakes, rivers, streams, monuments and crops. It's becoming a serious problem in North America.

As the rain falls, it dissolves a gas, carbon dioxide, from the air. This makes the rain slightly acidic. The rain then flows over the ground in streams. In some places the rock beneath the streams can be dissolved by the mildly acidic water. This type of rock is called limestone. The tiny bits of the limestone that dissolve are said to make the water hard. This doesn't mean that it would *feel* any harder than other water, but it does have certain effects that you might notice. Areas with no limestone will have soft water.

Kettle Fur?

REALLY?

Have a look inside your kettle.

If you live in a hard water area there will be a lining of "kettle fur" around the inside of the kettle. "Kettle fur" is white or yellow. It's part of the limestone that was dissolved in your water. When you boil the kettle, some water evaporates into the air, leaving limestone behind.

Be sure you clean that bath properly, Steven.

Living in a hard-water area is altogether too much work.

If you live in a hard-water area, you will need more soap powder to wash your clothes. Many laundromats in hard-water areas have a sign on the wall saying they have soft water supplied — which means you can save money by using less soap. Soap reacts with the limestone in hard water to make scum. This makes the white "tide mark" left around baths and sinks after you have washed yourself — even if you were already clean! Because some soap is making scum, you need extra soap before you can get a lather for washing with.

Have a go at the lather test experiment:

Fill the beakers with equal amounts of water so the test is fair.

Add a drop of liquid soap to each beaker of water. Shake after each drop. How many drops do you need to make a lather?

Hard Water

Distilled Water

Boiled Hard Water

Remember to boil the hard water several times.

If you live in a soft-water area, collect some hard water on a visit to a hard-water area.

You can buy distilled water at drugstores or grocery stores.

Write down the results of your experiment and compare them with those on the next page.

Now that you've tested the hardness of your water, you can wash the dishes. And then don't forget to dry them. Have you ever wondered why a towel dries things? Towels work rather like sponges. They soak up the water by capillary action. Water tends to rise up any narrow tube. The narrower the tube, the higher the water will rise. We call this capillary action. In a towel the tiny spaces between the threads of cloth act like narrow tubes and fill up with water. If you can find a narrow tube, a thin drinking straw will do, dip it in water and watch the water rise up inside it.

Some houses can get damp walls because of this capillary action. This is called rising damp. The water rises up from the ground through the tiny holes inside the bricks.

Similarly, water rises up the stems of plants by capillary action. Get a white carnation or a stalk of celery. Stand the cut end of it in some water that you have colored with dark food coloring. After a few hours you should see the darkened water rising up inside the stem of celery or into the petals of the carnation. The water rises by capillary action through narrow tubes, called xylem tubes, inside the plant stem.

Hey. It'll soon be blue.

Several hours later

The oldest type of water wheel was made of wood and had buckets or vanes around its outer rim.

Undershot Waterwheel

vanes

The force of the water pushes against the vanes, causing the wheel to rotate. An undershot water wheel means the water pushes the vanes from the bottom.

Whether it's hard or soft, river water is used to help you in many different ways before it reaches your taps. For hundreds of years, people have used our streams and rivers as a source of power. One way to get power from a river is to build a water wheel. The earliest records of water wheels were in China and Denmark in the first century BC. They spread rapidly throughout Europe in the Middle Ages. The Domesday Book, a record made by the Normans, tells us that England had 5,500 water wheels in 1086. That was almost two for each village. There are no similar records from other European countries, but the situation must have been the same throughout Europe. These water wheels were mainly used for grinding corn and mashing beer. Later, water wheels became important for running machines in spinning and weaving factories.

This is an overshot water wheel from about 1556. Overshot means the water comes from above.

This water wheel helped to power a rag and chain pump for mine drainage.

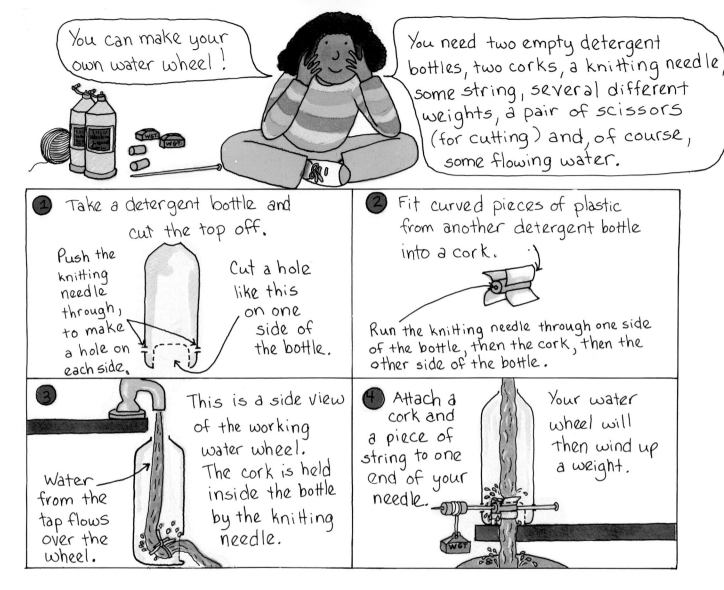

You can make your own water wheel!

You need two empty detergent bottles, two corks, a knitting needle, some string, several different weights, a pair of scissors (for cutting) and, of course, some flowing water.

1 Take a detergent bottle and cut the top off.

Push the knitting needle through, to make a hole on each side.

Cut a hole like this on one side of the bottle.

2 Fit curved pieces of plastic from another detergent bottle into a cork.

Run the knitting needle through one side of the bottle, then the cork, then the other side of the bottle.

3 Water from the tap flows over the wheel.

This is a side view of the working water wheel. The cork is held inside the bottle by the knitting needle.

4 Attach a cork and a piece of string to one end of your needle.

Your water wheel will then wind up a weight.

When you have built your water wheel, experiment by using it under different taps in your house. The most powerful tap will lift the biggest weight.

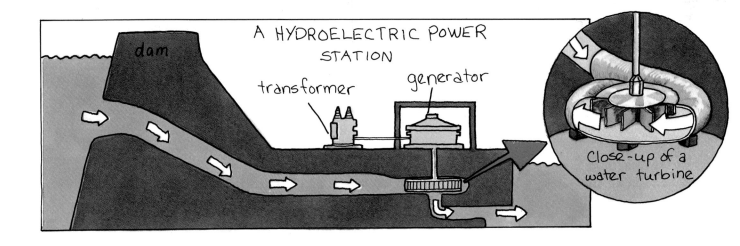

A HYDROELECTRIC POWER STATION

dam

transformer

generator

Close-up of a water turbine

Today, in hyroelectric power stations we use specially designed water wheels to make electricity. These are called turbines. Large dams are built to store the water that drives these turbines. Because of the high pressure of water behind the dams, they have to be very strong. They are thicker at the bottom where the pressure is greatest. As you go down deeper into water, the pressure increases. This is why deep-sea divers have to wear thick, strong pressure suits.

You can see the pressure in water by doing this simple experiment. All you need is a plastic bottle with three holes on one side - one at the top, one in the middle, and one at the bottom.

Then fill the bottle with water. Where in the bottle is the water pressure greatest? Check the answer below to see if you were right.

ANSWER: At the bottom.

Q: WHO INVENTED THE VERY FIRST STEAM ENGINE?

steam rushes out and pushes ball around

Fire heats up water inside boiler

A: Hero, an ancient Greek designed this steam engine in about AD 150. The course of history could have been changed if it had been used to drive machines.

For the past 300 years, we have also been gaining power from water by another means — the steam engine. In steam engines, water is heated to change it into steam, which moves a piston to produce power. The steam is then changed back to water again and recycled.

Q: WHO WAS MR. WATT?

A: Mr. James Watt was an inventor. He was a Scotsman who did lots of work producing early steam engines. He improved an existing engine built by Thomas Newcomen with a design of his own patented in 1769.

Engines designed by James Watt were used to power factory machines throughout the world. Even today, with most machines working on electricity, steam is still important. Power stations that produce our electricity burn coal or oil to heat steam, which then drives water wheel turbines. Even nuclear power stations heat steam to do the same job.

90 watts

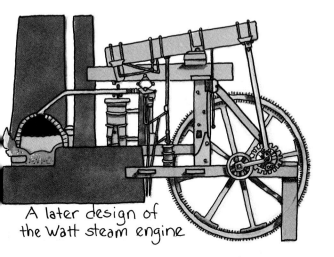

A later design of the Watt steam engine

Q: WHAT'S A WATT? A: It is a unit of power. 1 kilowatt equals 1,000 watts. This measurement of power is named after James Watt.

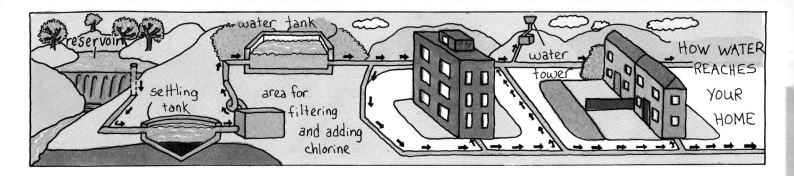

Even with all the work water does on the way to you, some of the water does complete its journey from the sea, through the clouds, rain and rivers to your taps. Many people in our world do not have such luxury. They can hardly dream of getting water just by turning a tap in their house — let alone water fit to drink!

To reach this pure state, our water is taken from the reservoirs, where it has been collected, to the waterworks. Here it stands in settling tanks, where the larger bits of unwanted material fall to the bottom. The water is then filtered, or strained, to remove the smaller bits of waste material.

You can make your own water filter, which will be similar to those at the waterworks, like this:

26

Water treated like this is now clean, but it is still not fit to drink because it may have germs in it that you cannot see. The germs are killed by adding to the water a small amount of a poisonous gas called chlorine. You will have smelled chlorine gas in pools, where it is also added to the water to kill germs. It can make your eyes sting.

The water is now clean and fit for you to drink straight from your tap. This is how your tap works:

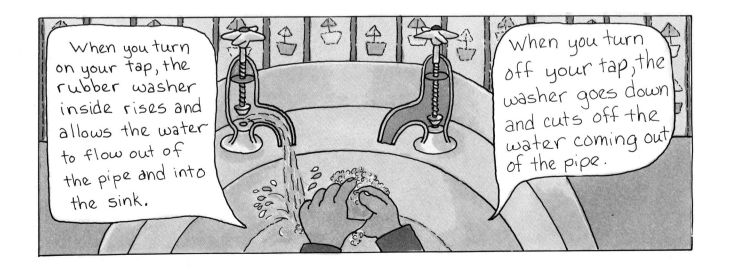

Around 1700 BC the Minoan Palace in Crete had piped water supplying baths, basins and latrines. The Romans, too, had lots of baths.

Reek! Reek!

But in most European countries, right up to the 1800s, hardly anybody washed themselves.

Phew. They must have reeked.

If you have a dripping tap, you should replace the washer. Large amounts of water are wasted every year by leakage. A hole the size of a pinhead in a main pipe can leak 720 quarts (680 l) an hour. That is about ten baths full of water! In Britain, where many water pipes are over 100 years old, nearly a quarter of all the collected water is lost.

Used water leaves your house through the drains. A lot, of course, goes down the toilet. Take a look inside your toilet tank to see how it works.

tank

handle

ball cock

water pipe

plunger

bowl of toilet

When you push the handle down, the plunger pushes up and forces water into the bowl. The ball cock, which floats on the water, goes down, and this makes more water go into the tank.

The first flushing toilet was invented by Sir John Harrington, an Englishman, in the 1590s.

In most developed countries, running water and efficient sewage and drainage systems did not exist until the 19th century.

Raw sewage passes down pipe

All the waste water from your house flows into the sewage system. This system also collects water from industry and from the streets after a rainfall. The used water then flows down to the sewage works. Used water contains oil, poisons, acids, detergents, sewage and even rags, wood, and plastics. These all have to be removed so that the seas and rivers are not polluted.

This is how the water is cleaned at the sewage works:

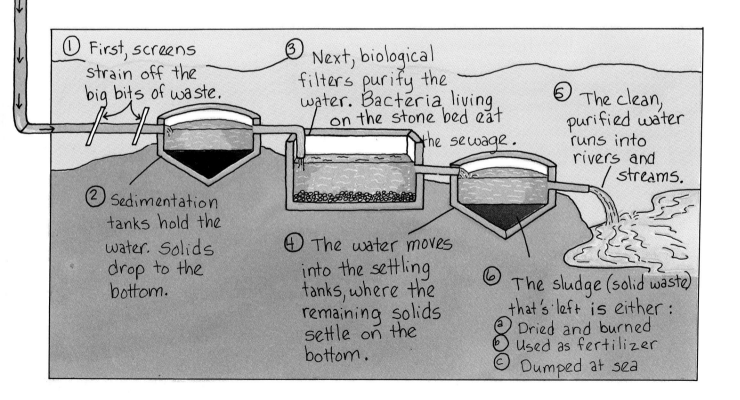

① First, screens strain off the big bits of waste.

② Sedimentation tanks hold the water. Solids drop to the bottom.

③ Next, biological filters purify the water. Bacteria living on the stone bed eat the sewage.

④ The water moves into the settling tanks, where the remaining solids settle on the bottom.

⑤ The clean, purified water runs into rivers and streams.

⑥ The sludge (solid waste) that's left is either:
ⓐ Dried and burned
ⓑ Used as fertilizer
ⓒ Dumped at sea

After treatment at the sewage plant, the cleaned water can be used again. Throughout the world, lots of people are drinking water that has already been used and purified many times.

Despite the cleaning of sewage, many of the Earth's water resources are polluted. Many of the world's large cities are only now beginning to clean up their rivers and waterways. We are still polluting the sea. Oil spilled at sea, in particular, can have terrible consequences. The oil floats on water and is brought to the coasts by wind and tides. It destroys beautiful beaches. It can cling to the feathers of sea birds, and they lose their waterproofing. Thousands of sea birds die each year from oil pollution. Pollution of the seas is a worldwide problem that will need cooperation and international action to solve.

If you find a bird with oil-polluted feathers, telephone your local bird sanctuary.

Many birds may die through eating polluted fish.

More than 150 people from Minamata Bay, Japan, died after eating fish polluted with mercury. A factory nearby was found to be discharging mercury into the bay.

We have followed water on its journey from the sea, through clouds, rain, rivers, all its various uses, and back to the sea again. The water has come full cycle.

Glossary

Acid rain: rain that has been polluted by sulfuric and nitric acid from industry.

Arid: when referring to geographic location, it usually indicates an area with little or no rain.

Buoyancy: the capacity to remain afloat in a liquid or to rise in air or gas.

Capillary action: the tendency for liquid to rise in a tube because of the force of its attraction to the sides of the tube.

Chlorine: a poisonous chemical used to bleach out colors and to purify water by killing germs.

Drought: a long period of dry weather.

Evaporate: change into a vapor.

Gravity: the force that attracts objects within the sphere of a celestial body (such as the Earth, Sun, or Moon) to its center.

Hard water: water containing dissolved material that keeps soap from bubbling.

Hydroelectricity: electricity that is made by running water.

Monsoon: a wind system that reverses its direction by the seasons, producing dry and wet seasons.

Plimsoll lines: marks on the hull of a ship that show how much it can legally and safely carry.

Reservoir: a body of water collected and stored in a natural or artificial lake, often to be used later for making electricity.

Sedimentation: the material deposited at the bottom of a liquid.

Steam engine: a machine that turns the heat energy of steam into power.

Tsunami: a series of terrible waves caused by an undersea volcanic blast or earthquake; can travel 12,000 miles without losing power.

Turbine: a water-powered machine run by a wheel that is put into motion by falling or running water.

Water vapor: the diffused gaseous state of water.

Watt: a unit, or measure, of electrical power.

Index

EDUCATION